HOW TO
GET A GUY
IN 10 DAYS

ISBN: 1-4196-5846-8

Acknowledgments

Jeannie and Michele would like to thank:

Our families for all their support and our
friends for all their inspiration.

Special thanks to:

Tyla Berchtold, Scott Leonard, Dorian Garcia
and Brian Alexander.

HOW TO GET A GUY IN 10 DAYS

written by

Michele Alexander & Jeannie Long

DAY
1

Meet him at a party.

Execute your skinny pose.

Say something funny,
and touch his arm.

Immediately ignore him.

Flirt and circulate.

Tell your friends you're bored
and leaving.

Make sure he's listening.

Make out with him, but leave
him wanting more.

Make your last booty call to
your ex.

DAY
2

When he calls, send it directly
to voicemail.

Keep yourself busy.

Go shopping.

When he calls again, tell him
you already have a date with
some guy. You'd break plans, but
you're way too nice to cancel
last minute.

Call your hottest guy friend and bribe him to be your date.

*Make sure he's not gay...he WILL KNOW.

Find out where he'll be.

Show up.

Act bored and flirt with him
across the bar.

Rendevous with him near the bathroom.

Tell him to call you later.

Turn off your phone.

DAY
3

Call and tell him your phone
wasn't charged.

Before he picks you up
for dinner, eat.

Wear something sparkly.

Remove all girlie magazines and replace with cerebral novels.

Suggest an inexpensive
restaurant.

At dinner, always be at least
one drink behind him.

Never interrupt him, even if he's boring you.

Make him think he's opening up
a whole new world for you.

Order something in the
mid-range price from the menu.

Don't finish it.

When he drops you off, don't
invite him in.

Tell him you have to get up
early and run a marathon.

DAY
4

Keep yourself busy.

Go shopping.

Max out your credit cards.

If he texts you, ignore it.

(Never communicate via text, act like you
don't know what it is)

Have a day of beauty with your friends.

(massage, steam, mani/pedi, facial)

Return his call.

Tell him you're sorry it's so late,
you've been busy all day
working out.

Suggest meeting somewhere.

(Make sure it's on your turf)

Accentuate your cleavage.

Accidentally flash him the new
garters you bought today.

Go to his place.

Excuse yourself and make a
quick break for his cd collection.

When you're making out, quote
Pat O'Brien.

Immediately get up and tell him
you've never been so turned on
in your whole life.

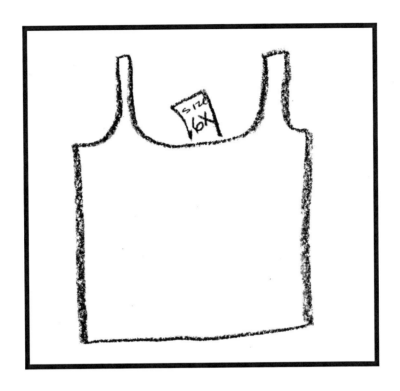

Leave behind an item of clothing with the smallest sized tag on it.

DAY
5

Tell him you're sorry about the blue balls. You just got scared and you want to make it up to him.

Invite him to your place.

Cook him dinner.

Show him your genealogy.

Insert Heidi Klum.

Constantly bend over and check the oven.

(Wear heels, a mini-skirt and a sexy apron)

Mention that you're an
old-fashioned girl who likes to
cook, clean and loves to iron.

Quote lines from
"The Godfather."

"Accidentally" have "Star Wars"
playing on the TV
when you turn it on.

Whatever you do, don't have sex.

DAY
6

Go out for a 'girl's night.'

Get it all out of your system.

Go to a buffet. Eat everything!
You're starving!

When getting into a club, refer
to your group as the "fun posse."

Dance on tables.

Flirt for free drinks.

Drive-thru Taco Bell.

Order one of everything.

Don't call him.

DAY
7

Only introduce him to your hot
friends with boyfriends.

"Accidentally" take him to a gay bar.

(This will ensure all eyes will be on you)

Stretch.

(So he can see your hot bod)

Let him lead the way.

(Even if he's going in the wrong direction)

Moisturize, so your skin
is baby soft.

Mention your ex-boyfriend is in town and wants to see you.

Tell him you can't wait until
summer when you can sunbathe
topless.

(It's the time you feel most free)

Remember, still no sex.

Tell him you're waiting for the right guy.

If he stays over, don't crowd
him in bed.

(No spooning, no cuddling, no canoodling)

DAY
8

Sneak out of bed in
the morning.

Freshen up and slip back in bed.

Wake him up and tell him you
have a big day ahead of you.

After he leaves,
go back to sleep.

When he calls, tell him you're busy and hate talking on the phone anyway.

Call your friends.

Talk about everything.

Invite the "fun posse" over
for a slumber party.

Call and ask him to come by.
It's super important.

Hide the pizza boxes and
change out of your sweatpants.

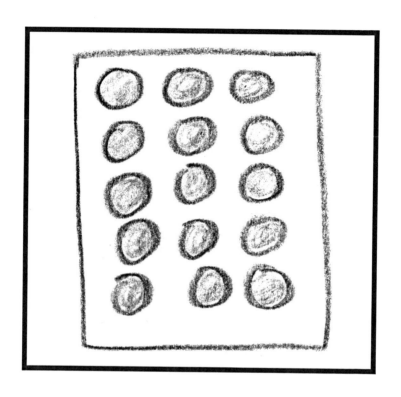

Lay out Twister.

Be 'left hand green, right hand blue' when he comes over.

Make him feel useful.

Ask if he'd like to stay
and spin the wheel.

DAY
9

Fake a break-in.

When he comes over, tell him
this is the first time in your life
you've ever really felt safe.

Show him how much you care.

Order the fight
on Pay-Per-View.

Tell him to invite his friends over.

Have lots of beer.

Even Ned the Ped.

DAY 10

Apply for "The Amazing Race"
together because you're
a risk taker and you guys
would never fight.

If he asks what you think about
marriage, tell him you don't.

Never mention "love,"
even when referring to people,
places or things.

Introduce him to his idol,
Chuck Norris.

Now you've got him.

Just act yourself.

(He'll get used to it)

Make love.

Tell him you love him.

Ask him when you're going to
get married.

Books also written by this author:

How to Lose a Guy in 10 Days
How to Tell He's Not the One in 10 Days
How to Get Over a Guy in 10 Days

Available on Amazon.com and other major booksellers.

For more information, please contact
HowToIn10Days@gmail.com.

Made in the USA